National Museums Scotland

Scotland's Vikings

Frances and Gordon Jarvie
with illustrations by Fhiona Galloway

SCOTTIES SERIES EDITORS
Frances and Gordon Jarvie

Contents

Second edition (revised) published in 2008
by NMS Enterprises Limited – Publishing
a division of NMS Enterprises Limited
National Museums Scotland
Chambers Street, Edinburgh EH1 1JF

Text © Frances and Gordon Jarvie 1997, 2008

Images © Trustees of the National Museums
of Scotland (except where noted to the
contrary)

ISBN (13): 978-1-905267-10-1
ISBN (10): 1-905267-10-X

**British Library Cataloguing in
Publication Data**
A catalogue record of this book
is available from the British Library.

Book design concept by Redpath.
Cover design by Mark Blackadder.
Illustration by Fhiona Galloway.
Layout by NMSE – Publishing.

Printed and bound in Slovakia by Tlačiarne BB.

CREDITS

Many thanks are due to the following
individuals and organisations who have
supplied images and photographs for this
publication:

FHIONA GALLOWAY
for all illustrations except where noted

NATIONAL MUSEUMS SCOTLAND
for all photographs except where noted

FRANCES JARVIE
for pages 10 (top), 11 (top) and additional
material

THE ÁRNI MAGNÚSSON INSTITUTE FOR
ICELANDIC STUDIES, REYKJAVÍK
Flateyjarbók, Gl. kgl. saml. 1005 fol., f. 76r.
14th century
Photographer: Jóhanna Ólafsdóttir
for page 21 (painting)

SHETLAND ISLANDS COUNCIL
for page 24 (above)

THE LIBRARY OF CONGRESS
for page 28

PATERSON, R. (maker) and NICOLAYSEN, N.
(draughtsman) for model ship on page 4

SCOTTIE BOOKS

For a full listing of NMS Enterprises
Limited – Publishing titles and related
merchandise:
www.nms.ac.uk/books

Who were the Vikings?

The Vikings were sea rovers who raided the coasts of Scotland from about AD 790. They came all the way from Scandinavia, which today is the countries known as Norway, Sweden and Denmark.

But the raids were not just in Scotland. The Vikings found that England, Ireland and Normandy in France were also easy targets for them to attack, so they did ....

Scandinavia is in the north of Europe (see maps on pages 8 and 31), so the Vikings were also known as the **Northmen** or **Norsemen** by their victims.

In their early raids on Scottish coasts, the Vikings were often very violent. They attacked, killed, and looted wherever they went.

The people of Scotland could only pray: 'From the fury of these Northmen, O Lord, deliver us!'

But we shall see in this book that the Vikings were not only wild warrior pirates ....

Farmers and settlers, traders and craftsmen soon followed the warriors across the North Sea from Scandinavia, and settled in parts of the country that we now call Scotland.

Take the test

Did Vikings have horns on their helmets?

Yes ☐ No ☐

Were the Vikings known only as pirates?

Yes ☐ No ☐

Answers on page 38

What's in a name?

The name **Viking** comes from the Norse word **vik**, meaning a **creek** or **inlet of the sea**. If you look at a map of the coast of Norway you will see that it is full of **creeks** or **fjords**. It was from these **fjords** that the Vikings sailed out in their long-ships.

3

'West-over-sea'

What made the Vikings undertake dangerous and difficult voyages across the seas rather than stay safely at home in their own lands?

There were a number of reasons. First, there were lots of wars at home in Scandinavia, between the Norwegian and Swedish and Danish kings and leaders. The people on the losing side might have been pushed out of their lands and forced to look for new homes elsewhere. Second, perhaps there were too many people in Scandinavia and not enough land for everyone.

Sailing skills

Vikings were great sailors and skilled navigators, so this is why the Vikings *sailed* to new lands. In those days the sea was the great highway. There were few roads and people rarely travelled by

Model of the Gokstad Viking ship, AD 860 (see p. 6).

Trade and money

Vikings had trade routes all over Europe, trading with people in England, France, Germany, and Asia in the east. Coins from these lands have been found in Scotland in Viking sites. Vikings did not use money as we do today. Coins, like these ones found in Orkney, were weighed as silver and given in return for goods (**bartering**).

land. Viking long-boats were built for speed, outsailing any others on the northern seas. From the coast of Norway they could reach Shetland and Orkney in two days with a good wind.

For glory and for loot ...

The peaceful life didn't appeal to the first Viking raiders: even their gods were warlike. They learned that some of the land to the west of Scandinavia ('west-over-sea' as they called it) was rich and poorly defended against attack. So they returned again and again in search of more loot.

… for land

Later on, the Vikings were looking for fertile land. If their own homelands were overcrowded, the young men would have followed the pirates west-over-sea in order to find new lands on which to start farms. We know they were skilled farmers, growing many crops, and keeping cattle, pigs, goats, sheep, horses and poultry.

… and for trade

The Vikings were also keen traders. They brought ship-loads of goods produced in their own countries (furs, timber, ropes) and sold them abroad. They also bought things abroad which they could sell for a profit at home, such as cloth, silk, wine and spices.

Activity

You are preparing your long-ship for a journey to Scotland. What should you take with you? Put these items in order of how important you think they might have been to a Viking, and explain why.

sword	axe
fresh water	flints
fruit	jewellery
bread	animals
warm clothes	barrels

If you could give a Viking one item from today's world, what might it be and why?

Answers and suggestions on page 38

Scales and weights

Vikings also used silver ingots or pieces of silver jewellery, like bits of bracelets, for trade. They weighed the silver to see how much it was worth and what they could exchange it for. Below is a set of Viking scales and seven weights found in the grave of a man at Kiloran Bay, Colonsay, in the Inner Hebrides. The weights and scales show that he was probably a trader.

Viking long-ships

For 400 years, from about AD 800 to 1200, the Vikings were the captains of the seas in northern Europe. They had the best ships and were masters of rudder, keel and sail.

The seas, oceans and great rivers were the highways of the world in Viking times. Transport by sea was easier, quicker and safer than overland travel. Vikings used long-ships that were swift and strong.

We know about Viking ships because archaeologists have found many buried in the ground. One of the most famous is the magnificent 23-metre-long Gokstad ship (see page 4), found in south-eastern Norway in 1881. Smaller boats have also been found and excavated at Scar and Westness in Orkney, and at Kiloran Bay in Colonsay.

The Gokstad ship, for example, was a fighting long-ship, sometimes called a **drakkar** or **dragon-ship**, because of the huge, grim-faced, painted dragon's head carved on the ship's front, or prow (see right).

Drakkars were longer and narrower than other ships of the time. With strong keels and large rectangular sails, the latest in rudder technology, and highly skilled crew-men, they simply out-performed any other ships on the high seas.

☑

Activity

This is the prow-head of the Gokstad ship. Design a prow-head for a fighting long-ship. You can make it as fierce as you like!

(The ship has been re-constructed at the Viking Ship Museum in Oslo, Norway.)

Drakkars did not need deep waters and could be sailed up the rivers of Europe. This meant that the Vikings were able to attack and capture many inland towns. Being lightweight, they could even be dragged overland between waterways. Without the dragon-ships, the **drakkars**, there would have been no Vikings outside Scandinavia.

Viking traders also had merchant ships called **knorrs**. **Knorrs** (see below) were often as long as the **drakkars**, but wider; they lay deeper in the water, especially when loaded. There was often a deck to cover the cargo and to keep it dry.

?

Mystery objects

Do you know what these objects are? Here's a clue: they are parts of a boat ... but which parts?

OBJECT
B

OBJECT
A

Answers on page 38

Off to Scotland!

Why did the Vikings come to Scotland in the first place?

It was the first land they saw …

If you look at the map below of the Viking world of 'west-over-sea', Lerwick in Shetland is less than 200 miles from Bergen in Norway. In other words, it was the first landfall the Vikings encountered. Shetland and Orkney were only two days' sail from the Norwegian coast. These places were used like stepping stones or staging posts for the Viking drakkars or knorrs on their travels. Here Viking crews could take on fresh supplies of food and water for their journeys down the west coast of Britain to the Hebrides, to the Isle of Man and to Dublin. Likewise, the Faeroe Islands and Iceland were stepping stones on the more northerly Viking routes to Greenland, and even as far as America.

What's in a name?

The Norse name for Cape Wrath is **Hverfa**. This means 'the Cape for turning round'.

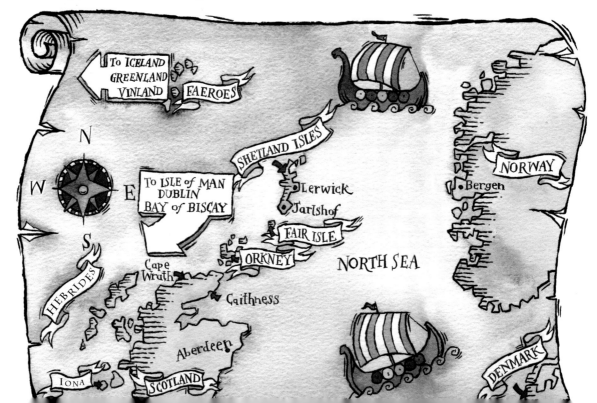

… it had good fertile land

Orkney has always had fertile farmland. It was attractive to the Norsemen looking for farmland over a thousand years ago – just as it is attractive to Orkney's cattle and grain farmers of today.

… oh, and lots of loot

The first Vikings were fearless pirates. Some of their favourite targets were monasteries and religious communities. There were many of these around the Scottish coasts. They were often on small, isolated offshore islands like Iona, so they were very easy to attack from the sea. They were easily looted. The precious church ornaments were often made of gold and silver. And the monks were not warriors – they were defenceless men of God.

? Mystery object

Do you know what this object is? Found on Culbinsgarth, Bressay, in Shetland, it was carved between the 9th and the 10th century. Can you see any animals in the design?

Answer on page 38

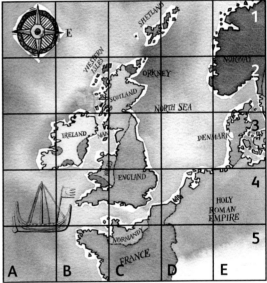

☑ Compass game

Follow the Vikings on their travels from Norway to Scotland and Europe by plotting 'Xs' on the map above. Start in Block E1. Steer a course to Normandy via Orkney and the Isle of Man. What co-ordinates do you need? (E1, D1, etc.)

Answers on page 38

9

The Vikings are here ...

'Viking long-ships have just attacked Holy Island off the coast of Northumberland. The monastery of Lindisfarne has been raided ...'

Above: The town crest of Crail in Fife, near the Isle of May, has a Viking long-ship on it.

In June of the year 793 Viking long-ships attacked Holy Island in Northumberland. They plundered and sacked the monastery of Lindisfarne. In 795 the rich and famous Celtic monastery on Iona suffered its first Viking attack. During a later attack on Iona, in 825, Vikings killed the abbot Blathmac for refusing to lead them to the precious shrine of the monastery's saint, Columba.

Sea raiders had the advantage of surprise. If they met with too much resistance, they jumped back into their boats and sailed away as swiftly and silently as they had come.

The Christian missionary Adrian was less famous than Columba of Iona. His base was a tiny priory on the Isle of May, at the entrance to the Firth of Forth.

A house in Crail in Fife is known as St Adrian's. It looks over the Firth of Forth to the Isle of May. This carving is set above the doorway of the house.

Activity

Imagine you are a journalist covering the Viking invasion at Lindisfarne. Make up your own newsflash report to send back to the television studio.

Above: Broch interior, at Glenelg, near Kyle of Lochalsh.

What's in a word?

The Scots word **broch** comes from the Old Norse word **borg**, a circular tower built from drystone. Drystone, which is a method of making walls without mortar (cement), was common in Scotland from the late Iron Age.

Adrian's mission was to convert the pagan Picts of Fife to Christianity. The Vikings attacked this defenceless community in 875, murdering Adrian and several of his followers. Nearly 300 years later Adrian was declared a saint, and pilgrims (who included several kings of Scotland) came to the Isle of May to worship at his shrine.

The warlike Pictish peoples of Orkney and Shetland were also hunters, farmers and fishermen. When attacked by Vikings, they often withdrew their livestock into brochs for protection. Archaeologists think Picts and Vikings eventually lived alongside each other in peace.

Soon the Northern Isles were Viking colonies, ruled by Norsemen, settled by Norsemen, using Norse language and laws. Norse settlements were also established in Caithness, Sutherland and the Western Isles. For the Vikings, Sutherland was their 'southern land'.

However, it was not only Scotland that felt the fury of the Vikings, who also captured large areas of England, Ireland and northern France. In 841 Rouen was captured, and it became the capital of Normandy ('land of the Northmen'). Dublin was also taken at that time; it became their chief trading port in the west. And they took York (Jorvik) in 866, making it their main trading town in England. Try to find some of these places on a good map of Northern Europe.

? Mystery object

This object is beautifully crafted. Dated to the 9th century, it was found on the Isle of Eigg. It is part of a bigger object. Do you know what it might be?

Answer on page 38

Warriors and weapons...

The Vikings who raided Scotland came from a warrior society. They knew how to work metal, as their tools and weapons prove.

All free Norsemen had a right to carry weapons. Even at home they would be likely to keep an axe or spear, or perhaps a sword.

Norse raiders in their long-ships were not just brave fighters; they were also well armed. Their swords were deadly weapons, as sharp edged as a razor. They also carried stout battle axes, and sometimes the axe head was decorated with a pattern.

They had strong wooden shields with which to defend themselves. They were often brightly coloured. Rich Viking warriors might wear an iron helmet for protection, and some wore chain-mail over their tunics.

Activity

Imagine you are a Viking metal-worker making shields for the warriors. Design a shield and write the name of your warrior or his nickname on it. Use your own name, if you like. Try writing the name in the runic alphabet (see page 19).

Archaeologists have found examples of helmets, shields and chain-mail in the graves of Vikings. Before the Vikings became Christians, their weapons were often buried around them, to offer protection when they went into **Valhalla**, 'the hall of the gods'.

Viking metalworkers also made wonderful jewellery and ornaments. And they were very good tool-makers.

Looking good

Below is a beautiful example of the craft of jewellery-making. It was not made by a Norse craftsman, however, but is a Celtic brooch found in a Viking grave, and discovered in 1963 on an Orkney farm. It is known as the Westness brooch. Here is how the brooch would have been worn. Can you find any animals among the designs on this brooch?

Answer on page 38

?

Mystery man

Have you any idea who this mystery man is? Here is a clue: he's a warrior and he's part of a game … and he appears to be *very* annoyed. Find out why on pages 18 and 38.

Settlers and farmers...

'Dear Dad
Having a great time here in Scotland. There's a lot of good farmland and it's not too crowded .... '

The early Viking raiders probably liked what they saw of Scotland. The word went back to Scandinavia that there was good farmland, and it was not over-crowded nor heavily defended against incomers.

Soon there were Viking settlements and farms. Many Viking settlers married local girls and became part of the local com-munities. In Orkney and Shetland, Norse was soon the language of all the islands. But in the Western Isles the Norse settlers ended up speaking Scots Gaelic, perhaps because fewer Norsemen settled there.

One of the best-preserved Viking farm-steads in the British Isles is **Jarlshof** on Shetland. It was excavated in the 1930s when archaeologists uncovered a succession of settlements. We know the Vikings lived here from about AD 800.

The original settlement had a long-house, or farmhouse, shown in this picture. Next to it was a small building which may have been used as a bath-house or sauna. Then came the black-smith's workshop, where tools and weapons were made or mended. The raiders still needed their swords!

📄 Fast fact

Vikings lived to be about 30 years old on average. Very few lived to the age of 50. Sadly many Viking children did not live beyond the age of five years old.

The picture below shows how Jarlshof might have looked in about 1200. The original community had flourished over a period of 400 years. There were new buildings, walls, roads, even pavements. Fishing was a major activity, and passing long-ships would have stopped here for food and water.

Few weapons have been found at Jarlshof. The fish-hooks, sickles and scythes that do exist tell us that the folk living there were not warriors. Their lives revolved around their farms: planting and harvesting crops like barley, oats, wheat and vegetables, tending the animals for meat and milk as well as wool and leather for clothes. All garments were home-made: tunics and loose trousers for the men, long dresses and pinafores for the women, cloaks for colder weather, and with leather boots or shoes.

Other Viking houses have been excavated in Orkney, South Uist and in Caithness.

Jarlshof settlement around AD 1200.

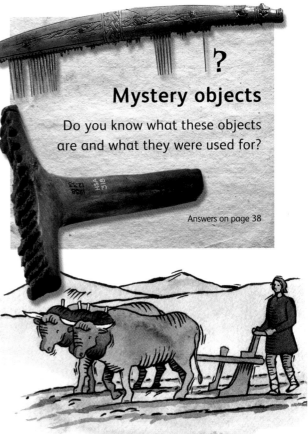

? Mystery objects

Do you know what these objects are and what they were used for?

Answers on page 38

Viking beliefs

The first Viking invaders of Scotland were pagans. Many of their gods and goddesses were warlike and, according to Norse legend, they lived in a place called **Valhalla**, or the **hall of the gods**.

Vikings who had died gloriously in battle were thought to be transported to **Valhalla** to feast with the gods. There they would be cared for by warrior maidens, known as the **Valkyries**. Three of the Norse gods were **Odin** (sometimes called **Woden**), **Thor** and **Frigga**.

When they died, Vikings sometimes cremated their chiefs in their long-ships. The long-ship would be transformed into a funeral pyre and set alight. Sometimes it was launched out to sea. This form of cremation was believed to send the dead person instantly to Valhalla.

Odin

The greatest and oldest of the Norse gods. All other gods obeyed him. He was the god of wisdom, poetry and battle, and he had many nicknames: **The One-eyed**, because he exchanged the other eye for the gift of knowledge and wisdom; **The All-knowing**, because his two black ravens **Mind** and **Memory** (**Hugin** and **Munin**), brought him daily news of all that was happening in the world; and **The Lord of the Gallows**, because he had the power to make hanged men tell him all their secrets after death.

Thor

Thor was one of **Odin**'s sons. He was the god of thunder, storms, and controlled the winds. Viking crews prayed to **Thor** before their long-ships set out on a voyage. His sign was a great hammer, which he used for braining giants.

Frigga

Wife of **Odin**, she was goddess of married love and the family hearth. Sometimes she is confused with **Freya**, goddess of beauty and the night, and **Freya**'s brother **Frey**, god of fertility.

UP HELLY AA

Other Vikings were buried in graves, and Viking-age cemeteries have been found at Westness (Orkney), Valtos (Lewis) and elsewhere.

In 1991 an important excavation at Balnakeil in Sutherland uncovered a 12-year-old boy buried with a full range of military equipment. Was he perhaps the son of a Viking chief? Would he need weapons in the next world? Or were they placed in the grave to help him make the journey from childhood to manhood?

Fast fact

The whalebone plaque (right) may have been used for smoothing fine cloth which would have been stretched over the plaque to dry with a lump of smooth, warm glass. 'Ironing' had arrived!

What's in a name?

The Norse gods have given their names to three of our weekdays – **Odin's** day, **Thor's** day, and **Frigga's** day. Can you work out which days these are?

Answers on page 38

Another discovery in 1991 was a Viking boat burial in sand dunes on the shoreline at Scar in Orkney. Grave goods included a fine sword, quiverful of arrows, large bone comb, fine brooch, pile of gaming pieces, pair of shears, and a decorative whale-bone plaque. This was thought to have been a betrothal gift carved by a young man during the long winter evenings and given to his beloved as part of a marriage proposal.

VIKING BOAT BURIAL

WHALEBONE PLAQUE

17

Art and writing

'The year is 1831 … a major art discovery has just been announced …. 93 chess-pieces, carved in walrus ivory, have been found in the sand dunes on the west coast of Lewis.'

Above: Five of the eleven Lewis chessmen in the National Museums Scotland. The rest are in the British Museum, London. The **berserker** is the one who is biting his shield.

This was a very important and exciting discovery indeed: a magnificent collection of gaming pieces, carved in about AD 1150.

What's in a word?

Why is the warrior on page 13 (the second chesspiece on the right, above) biting his shield? Viking warriors put on the skin of a fearless animal like a bear or wolf to make them feel brave before battle. They then danced about, yelling, howling and biting their shields, working themselves into a sort of battle-frenzy, driving themselves **berserk**! In Norse **berserk** simply means **bear-shirt** (the garment warriors put on before battle). Remember the Vikings next time you hear that someone has **gone berserk.**

? Mystery object

Do you know what animal this charm or amulet is made from? It is made from its tooth, with runes carved on it. The amulet is from the Brough of Birsay, Orkney, AD 850-1200.

Answer on page 38

The **Runic alphabet**, used by the Vikings, was carved on wood, stone or bone. It was easier to carve straight lines than curves on these hard surfaces. See the alphabet at the top of the next page.

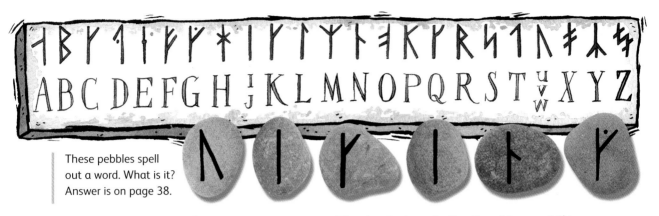

These pebbles spell out a word. What is it? Answer is on page 38.

Code-breaker

We know the Vikings used lots of nicknames. Using the code-breaker above, try writing these names in runes: Sigurd Silk-Beard, Olaf Flat-Nose, Brenda Starry-Eyes, Ingibiorg Seal-Head.

Give yourself a nickname which describes you best. Design your own Viking book-mark with your name and nickname written on it in runes.

Maes Howe, Orkney, with examples of the graffiti.

The best place in Scotland to see Viking runes is Maes Howe in Orkney, an ancient burial chamber built about 5000 years ago. It's even older than the Pyramids of Egypt. In about 1150, when Maes Howe was already 4000 years old, Norsemen raided the tomb looking for loot. Like typical vandals they left runic graffiti on the walls of this burial chamber. It's still there. Many of the carvings are personal names (like modern graffiti), followed by '**RR**' for '**reist runar**' (meaning 'carved' or 'cut these runes').

We read of Ingibiorg, the fair widow of Thorni, who slept here, and Helgi who carved here, and Hakon who took treasure from this mound. It says: 'These runes were carved by the man most skilled in runes in the western ocean, with the axe owned by Gauk Trandilson in the south land [or Iceland]'. It also tells us that some raiders had been on crusades to the Holy Land.

Vivid drawings were also carved: a lion, a slavering dog, a walrus, and a knotted serpent. See page 26 for a particularly unusual Maes Howe animal.

19

Viking timeline

AD 795	First Viking attack on Iona.	
800	Viking settlement at Jarlshof;	
800-900	Norse immigrants and settlers arrive in Scotland.	
825	Blathmac, abbot of Iona, killed.	
875	Killing of Adrian, missionary on Isle of May.	
c.900-1300	Norse earldom of Orkney.	
995	Earl Sigurd forced to adopt Christianity by King Olaf.	
1014	Battle of Clontarf, Dublin; Earl Sigurd killed.	
1048	Earl Thorfinn appoints Orkney's first bishop; church on Brough of Birsay.	
from 1100	Viking castles of Old Wick, Caithness; and Cubbie Roo's, at Wyre, Orkney.	
1117	Murder of Earl Magnus.	
1137	Building of St Magnus Cathedral, Kirkwall begun.	
c.1150	Lewis chesspieces carved.	
1150-51	Maes Howe tomb graffiti.	
1151-53	Earl Rognvald's pilgrimage to the Holy Land.	
1263	Battle of Largs.	
1266	Treaty of Perth: Norwegians give over Western Isles and Isle of Man to Alexander III of Scotland.	
1286-90	Maid of Norway briefly becomes Queen of Scots.	
1398-99	Henry Sinclair, 1st Sinclair earl of Orkney, voyages to North America following routes of Norsemen.	
1446	William Sinclair, Earl of Orkney, builds Roslin Collegiate Chapel near Edinburgh.	
1469	Orkney and Shetland given up by Denmark to James III of Scotland as part of marriage dowry.	

Kings and Queens of Scotland

1016-34	Malcolm II reigned
1058-93	Malcolm III ('Canmore')
1107-24	Alexander I
1124-53	David I ('The Saint')
1165-1214	William the Lion
1214-49	Alexander II
1249-86	Alexander III (see silver penny above)
1286-90	Margaret, Maid of Norway
1306-29	Robert I ('The Bruce')
1460-88	James III

Kings of Norway

c.900-45	Harald Finehair (see illustration above)
995-1000	Olaf Tryggvason
1015-30	Olaf Haraldsson ('St Olaf')
1093-1103	Magnus Bareleg
1223-63	Haakon IV ('The Great')

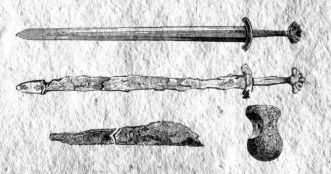

The Wider World

AD 793	Viking attack on Holy Island, Northumberland and the monastery of Lindisfarne.
c.800	Viking settlers arrive in Faeroe Islands.
874	First Viking settlement in Iceland.
911	Vikings granted lands in Normandy under Rollo.
930	Althing or Parliament of Iceland established.
986	Eric the Red founds Viking colony in Greenland.
1000	Leif Erikson's long-ships reach Vinland (Newfoundland).
1016	Cnut (Canute) is king of Denmark.
1028	Cnut is king of Norway, England, lord of Sweden.
1035-42	Cnut's sons are kings of England.
1066	Normans (descendants of Norsemen) take over in England after victory at the Battle of Hastings.

Norman Castle

1492	Christopher Columbus discovers America.

Viking sagas

The Vikings were great storytellers. The first stories or **sagas** were handed down by word of mouth from one generation to the next.

Snorre Sturlasson – one of the greatest recorders of sagas.

Myths and legends were mixed with history and memorised by the poets of the community. But by 1200 the sagas started to be written down by historians like Snorre Sturlasson in Iceland.

One of the earliest written sagas is *The Orkneyinga Saga*, a 'History of the Earls of Orkney'. It tells the story of Viking Orkney and Caithness from about 850 until 1150. It provides us with a lot of information about the Viking way of life.

The sagas help us to understand how the Vikings were slowly drawn away from their Norse culture and into the society and culture of Scotland, often by marrying Scots. They also tell us how they were converted to Christianity and gave up the old Norse gods.

Norse storytellers were called **skalds**. They were respected and well-paid men. As well as reciting sagas, they composed and sang ballads about warriors' successes in battle. Before battle the **skald** had to compose a suitable poem, maybe asking for help from the gods. **Skalds** were like the later Highland bards, who wrote poetry in praise of the Clan chiefs.

As the population of the Viking lands in Scotland slowly increased, more and more Viking families settled and lived together. The communities needed leaders. These were usually brave warriors who were also wealthy land-owners. The Norsemen called them **jarls**. We call them **earls**.

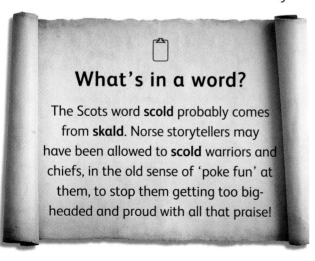

What's in a word?

The Scots word **scold** probably comes from **skald**. Norse storytellers may have been allowed to **scold** warriors and chiefs, in the old sense of 'poke fun' at them, to stop them getting too big-headed and proud with all that praise!

Over the next few pages we will take a look at parts of *The Orkneyinga Saga,* to see what it tells us about the Orkney **jarls** or **earls**.

☑
Fast fact

Viking surnames were created in a different way to Scots ones. For example, if a Viking called **Olaf** had a son called Erik, his surname would be **Erik Olafson**. If **Olaf** had a daughter called Kirsten, she would be **Kirsten Olafsdottir** (**Olafs-daughter**). What would your surname be, if you were a Viking?

Illustration from *Njáls saga*. This Norse saga comes from Iceland and is dated *c.*1350.

First saga of the Orkney jarls

It is AD 900 .... Harald Finehair is the king of Norway. He has just made his follower Sigurd the first earl of Orkney. Sigurd now controls Orkney on behalf of the king.

The coat of arms of Shetland, with the motto, 'By law shall the land be built up'. (Old Norse)

The main Norse earldom in Scotland was based on Orkney. Sigurd and his successors were earls (or jarls) of Orkney for over three hundred years, ruling over Shetland and Caithness as well as Orkney.

The sagas tell us that in 995 the earl of Orkney was another Sigurd – Sigurd the Stout, a mighty warrior. One day he had a surprise visit from Olaf Tryggvason, king of Norway at that time. Olaf was returning to Norway from a war cruise and had recently become a Christian. Capturing Sigurd and some of his men, Olaf gave him no choice. Become a Christian or die! Sigurd was at the king's mercy, so he became a Christian.

Sigurd the Stout died in 1014 in Ireland, on the battlefield at Clontarf outside Dublin, helping the Viking king of Dublin against the Irish king Brian Boru. Brian's army won and the Vikings were thrown out of Dublin after a great slaughter. Viking warriors from Orkney and Caithness, from Iceland, the Faeroes and the Hebrides, died at Clontarf.

Sigurd's son, Thorfinn the Mighty, became earl. It was Thorfinn who built a fine church at Birsay, and established Orkney's first bishop there. Today Birsay has some remains of Norse long-houses, or halls, built for chiefs like Thorfinn.

The death of Sigurd the Stout on the battlefield of Clontarf.

About fifty years after the death of Thorfinn, two cousins jointly inherited the earldom of Orkney. Earl Haakon and Earl Magnus were both grandsons of Thorfinn, and they soon became rivals. In April 1116 they agreed to meet on the small Orkney island of Egilsay to try to sort out their differences.

The saga tells us that each earl was to come with two boats and an equal number of unarmed followers to the island. Magnus arrived on the agreed day with his two ships. Then Haakon appeared – with eight ships and a large number of heavily armed warriors. He had tricked Magnus, whom he despised.

Magnus was killed by an axe-blow to the head and his body was taken to Birsay for burial at the church built by his grandfather, Thorfinn.

Soon stories of miracles were told about Magnus. Sick people who had prayed at his grave were cured; strange lights were seen in the sky. The bishop of Orkney began the process which led the Pope to declare Magnus a saint of the Church.

Years later the earldom passed to Magnus's nephew, Earl Rognvald. In 1137 he began to build a cathedral at Kirkwall dedicated to his murdered uncle. When Magnus's remains were removed from Birsay for reburial at the cathedral, a great cleft was found in his skull, probably made by a weapon cracking down on its victim's head. Here was gruesome archaeological evidence that the saga of the death of St Magnus was in fact true.

St Magnus Cathedral in Orkney today.

Second saga of the Orkney jarls

Here is another saga story about the same Earl Rognvald. This time we are told about how he took a party of Norsemen on a pilgrimage to the Holy Land in 1151.

The voyage from Norway to Jerusalem in the Holy Land included many adventures, including a winter stopover on Orkney, the storming of a Moorish castle in Spain, and the capture of a Saracen treasure ship near Sardinia. We also learn that Earl Rognvald and his companion, known as Sigmund Fish-Hook, swam in the river Jordan.

On Orkney, the Maes Howe graffiti tells us how these pilgrims (so-called 'Jerusalem-farers') opened the sacred grave mound in search of treasure. It appears to have been difficult for Earl Rognvald to keep this unruly bunch of adventurers under control!

Mystery animal

One of the pilgrims was a fine artist. He carved the above stone at Maes Howe (see page 19). What kind of animal do you think it is? Was it a beast that he expected to encounter on his crusade?

Answer on page 38

Fast fact

Scots call the Hebrides the Western Isles. Norsemen called them the Southern Isles. As on Orkney, Vikings established a bishopric here: with a bishop of **Sodor** and **Man** in charge. **Sodor** is Latin for the **Southern Isles**. The bishop of the Isle of Man still holds this title today.

Lords of the Isles

The Great Seal of King William the Lion (about 1165), showing him as a knight on horseback.

The seaways through the Hebrides were the Vikings' route south to their kingdoms of Man and Dublin, and other settlements around the Irish Sea, so these routes were important to them. The first Viking kingdom of the Western Isles was based on the Isle of Man. Its king, Godred of Man and the Hebrides, was a powerful vassal of the Norwegian crown. However, after his death in 1095, his territory broke up into smaller lordships.

One of the key figures in the 12th century was Somerled. His Norse mother was daughter of Godred of Man, but his Celtic father had kinship with the Scots kings. **Somerled**'s Norse name is **Sumar-lidi**, meaning **summer traveller**, the season when Norsemen went looting in their long-ships. (In Gaelic the name is **Somhairle**; in modern English it is **Sorley**.)

Somerled's base was probably on Islay, and he took the title of **Regulus** (ruler, or sub-king) of Argyll. His grandson Donald is regarded as the founder of the clan MacDonald, who took the title of Lord of the Isles.

Kings of Norway made occasional visits to these part-Gaelic part-Norse Lords of the Isles, to assert their authority over their territories and people. In 1098 King Magnus III 'Bareleg' came from Norway to the Western Isles on such a visit, burning and looting as he went, sparing only the island of Iona. He also made a treaty with the king of Scots, William the Lion.

They agreed that the mainland was Scotland, and that the kings of Norway should only own those islands they could sail around in their long-ships. According to the sagas, Magnus Bareleg also wanted Kintyre as Norse territory. Kintyre is not quite an island, but Magnus told his men to drag his long-ship across the narrowest part of the Kintyre peninsula, thus claiming it for himself because he had, in effect, *sailed* around it.

27

Norse names in Scotland

Fingal's Cave, Staffa, off the west coast of Scotland.

Dugald, Fingal, Finlay and Lachlan are all names that have Viking connections. Read on … perhaps your name has come from Norse roots as well.

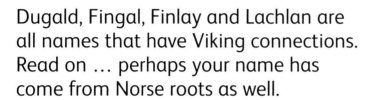

The name **Dugald** originally meant **dark stranger** (**dubh ghal**) in Gaelic, the nickname given by the Gaels to the Danish Vikings. The Gaelic nickname for a Norwegian Viking was **fair stranger** (**fionn ghal**), hence the Gaelic name **Fingal** (as in **Fingal's Cave**: see the picture at the top of the page).

Lochlann was the Norse word for Scandinavia, the **land of the lochs**; hence the Gaelic boy's name **Lachlan**. From such roots the clan names **MacLachlan** and **MacDougall** came about (**Mac** means **son of** in Gaelic).

Here are some Highland surnames which have come from Norse origins:

– **Finlay** (from **fionn ladh** or **fair hero**)
– **Gunn** (**Gunni** or **Gunnor** are Norse first names)
– **MacAskill** (from the Norse first name **Asketill**, the **sacred kettle** or **vessel of the gods**)
– **MacCorquodale** (from Norse **Thorketill**, the **sacred kettle of Thor**)
– **MacIver** (**Ivarr** was a Norse personal name)
– **MacKettrick** (from a Norse personal name **Sitrig**, meaning **true victory**)
– **MacLeod** (probably **son of the ugly wolf**)

Lots of Scottish place names are also from Norse. For example, the Norse word for an **island** is **ey**. Thus:

- **Colonsay** means **Columba's ey**
- **Jura** means **deer ey**
- **Raasay** means **roe-deer ey**
- **Orkney** means **boar's ey**
- **Hoy** means **high ey**
- **Westray** means **western ey**
- **Rousay** means **Rolf's ey**
- **Pabbay** means **priest's ey**
- South **Ronaldsay** means **Rognvald's ey**
- **Egilsay** means **church ey**
- **Rothesay** means **Ruari's ey**. The original island was Rothesay castle, surrounded by its moat (see page 30).

What's in a name?

Dingwall (Easter Ross), the villages of **Tinwald** (near Dumfries) and **Tingwall** (Shetland), hill of **Tynwald** (Isle of Man) and field of **Thingvellir** (Iceland) are place names with something in common. They were all sites of a Viking **thing** (pronounced **ting**), a local parliament which met to make laws, settle arguments and arrange ownership of the land.

Activity

Have you heard of the expression '**to pay through the nose**' for something? Where do you think this came from?

S	R	N	E	I	L	F	N	G	A
F	L	A	D	N	E	R	B	K	S
Y	H	L	N	C	I	R	E	J	W
O	M	L	E	A	I	B	C	Q	I
A	K	A	Y	T	L	C	E	W	V
Q	I	N	G	R	I	D	F	Y	O
P	A	C	B	N	D	H	G	F	R
Q	G	B	X	N	U	L	O	A	G
E	N	W	I	B	E	S	O	L	N
L	I	U	Q	R	O	T	C	O	I

Word search

Lots of Scots have first names which were once Norse names. Can you spot these names in the above word search?

Eric, Olaf, Magnus, Ingrid, Inga, Neil, Ranald, Torquil, Ivor, Brenda

We know the Norse word for a bay or creek was **vik**. The word **Vikings** means the **men of the creeks**. You can spot this in place names such as **Lerwick** (**muddy bay**), **Brodick** (**broad bay**), **Arisaig** (from a person's name – **Aros's vik**), **Wick** and **Nigg**. Other Norse words for bays and inlets of the sea are **voe** and **flow**, hence **Sullom Voe** and **Scapa Flow**.

A Norse word for a farm was a **byr** (modern Scots **byre**). Place names from this are **Canonbie** (the **canon's farm**), **Golspie** (**Galli's farm**), **Humbie** (**Hundi's farm**), and **Lockerbie** (**Lockhart's farm**).

Answer on page 38

Europe and the Vikings

By the year AD 1100 the nations of Europe were beginning to emerge, but what did Scotland look like at this time?

The Great Seal of King Alexander II (about 1214).

European countries had similar territories to those they occupy today. Scandinavia had the kingdoms of Norway, Sweden and Denmark. The kingdoms of England, Scotland, Ireland and France were known as West-over-sea.

Scotland was a strong kingdom by 1100, and its borders were more or less as they are today. A Scottish national culture was emerging under kings like Malcolm Canmore, William the Lion, and the three Alexanders. Scotland was a mixture of Pictish, Celtic and Viking influences to the north and west, with Strathclyde Britons to the south-west and Angles to the south-east.

King William the Lion (1165-1214) took back control of Caithness, Sutherland and Ross and Cromarty from the Vikings. King Alexander II (1214-49) took back Kintyre and the islands of Bute and Arran in the Clyde. To defend these new parts

of his kingdom from the Norsemen, Alexander built a strong castle at Rothesay. But in 1230 the long-ships returned to Bute and Norse warriors besieged the castle of Rothesay. They managed to cut their way through the soft red sandstone of the castle's outer wall, and then regained control in Bute for a while.

Two parts of today's Scotland remained firmly Norse. The Western Isles were ruled by the Norse Lords of the Isles, and Orkney and Shetland were governed by the Norse jarls of Orkney. Both of these chiefs were subjects of the king of Norway, not Scotland. The Scots kings Alexander II and III tried to buy the Western Isles, but their offers were firmly rejected by the Norwegian kings.

☑
Activity

Look at a map of modern Europe and compare it to the political map below. Can you spot any differences?

Answers and suggestions on page 39

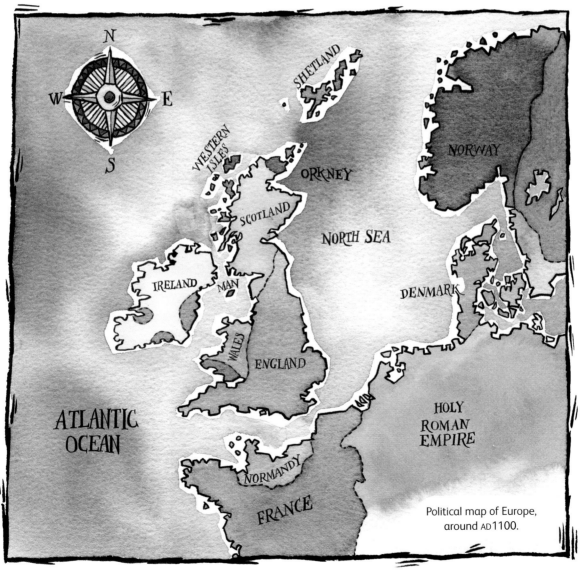

Political map of Europe, around AD1100.

Largs
The last battle

It is 1263. Haakon's fleet wait in the shelter of Lamlash Bay, on the Isle of Arran, for the Scots king Alexander III and his army. Suddenly a storm erupts …

Above: This iron and steel sword dates from this time period, the 13th century. It was found during excavations in the Isle of Man.

One of the greatest of all the Norse warrior kings was Haakon IV. For Haakon the Hebrides were part of the realm of Norway, not Scotland. To remind people of this he put on a show of strength and led a huge fleet of 150 long-ships from Bergen west-over-sea to Orkney.

King Haakon wanted to show his chieftains in the Western Isles that he was still their boss. He also wanted to show the king of Scots that he could and would control the Hebridean islands, by force if necessary. From Orkney, Haakon's great war-fleet sailed around Cape Wrath and south to the Hebrides.

They passed the narrow strait of water now called Kyle Akin, keeping Skye (still Norse territory) to westward.

The Norse fleet assembled in the shelter of Lamlash Bay on Arran.

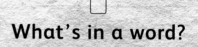

What's in a word?

Kyle Akin is a Gaelic name which means **Haakon's strait**.
Can you find it on a map?

Haakon wanted to negotiate with Alexander, who was waiting in Largs with his army. Sailing up the Firth of Clyde, the Norse fleet moored offshore at Largs. Then an October storm drove some of their ships on to the rocky foreshore. When the Norsemen tried to salvage their cargo, the Scots attacked them.

There was a fierce battle on the shore among the stranded long-ships. Many men died. Both sides thought they had won in the end, but as the Norsemen were eventually driven off, the Scots were probably right to claim the victory.

It was now too late in the season for Norse campaigns. Haakon, by then a sick man with a crippled fleet, planned to spend the winter on Orkney. He stayed at Kirkwall in the bishop's palace beside the fine new cathedral of St Magnus. He visited the saint's shrine, but found no cure for him there. Before winter set in, Haakon died and was laid to rest in the cathedral.

In the spring of 1264 Haakon's mighty flagship returned from Scapa Flow to Bergen, bearing the remains of the last of the great Viking sea-kings. Two years later, by the Treaty of Perth (1266), Haakon's successor sold the Hebrides and the Isle of Man to the king of Scots. Only Orkney and Shetland then remained Norse.

Margaret, Maid of Norway...

Alexander III was the last Celtic king of the House of Canmore to rule Scotland. When he died in 1286 his three-year-old grand-daughter Margaret, the Maid of Norway, took his place.

The Great Seal of King Alexander III (about 1265).

Alexander III's reign had been peaceful after the battle of Largs, and his kingdom prospered. But when he died in 1286 Scotland's royal dynasty was at an end. Of Alexander's family, only his three-year-old grand-daughter Margaret, the Maid of Norway, survived him.

Margaret's father was King Eric II of Norway (grandson of Haakon IV). Her mother had been Margaret, daughter of Alexander III of Scotland. So Margaret the Maid could have ruled two kingdoms.

Foreseeing the problem his death would cause, King Alexander had decreed that his grand-daughter should inherit the Scottish crown at his death. The Scots nobility were asked to agree to honour this arrangement. The king knew that otherwise they would squabble over the crown themselves, and bring civil war to Scotland.

Alexander died suddenly in 1286 after a fall from his horse. Scots ambassadors then sailed to Norway to invite Margaret to be their queen. Six guardians were appointed to rule the country until she grew up. In 1290, aged eight or nine, the young Maid of Norway sailed to Orkney before completing the journey to Scotland to inherit her crown.

and Queen of Scots

We are told Margaret was a poor sailor and that the seas were rough. In the end she never reached mainland Scotland. She died that winter at Kirkwall in Orkney, as her great ancestor King Haakon IV had done 26 years earlier.

The death of the young Maid of Norway led to a period of great turmoil for Scotland, as Alexander III had foreseen. The close links between Norway and Scotland, which had been forged by the Vikings, now began to loosen.

Fast fact

The deaths of Alexander III and the Maid of Norway were disastrous for Scotland. Can you find out why?

Answer on page 39

Below is part of an old Scots ballad. It is not known who Sir Patrick Spens was; or which king sat in 'Dunfermline toun'. Some say the poem is about the fateful journey of the Scots ambassadors when they brought home the Maid of Norway. You can read the whole poem in a book of Scots ballads.

The king sits in Dunfermline toun
        Drinking the blude-red wine,
'O where will I get a skeely skipper
        To sail this ship of mine?'

The king has written a braid letter
        And sealed it with his hand,
And sent it to Sir Patrick Spens
        A-walking on the strand.

To Noroway, to Noroway,
        To Noroway o'er the faem,
The king's dochter o Noroway,
        'Tis thou maun bring her hame.

The end of Norse power

Above: The armorial shield of the clan Gunn.

By 1469 Norway's kings were subjects of the kings of Denmark who were not interested in the remaining Norse territories west-over-sea – Orkney, Shetland, Faeroe and Iceland.

Several of the Norse earls (or jarls) of the premier earldom of Orkney had married Scots women and eventually the earldom passed out of Norse hands. In 1379 it went to Henry Sinclair, a Norman Scot with lands at Roslin, Midlothian. As Admirals of Scotland, the Sinclairs carried on the sea-faring tradition of the Norse earldom well into the 15th century.

There is an interesting story, backed by some evidence, that in 1398-99 Henry Sinclair and an Italian navigator called Niccolo Zeno followed the Norse sea-routes across the North Atlantic Ocean to Newfoundland and Nova Scotia, exploring as far south as Massachusetts.

They are said to have spent a winter living at peace among the Micmac Indians – ninety years before the famous explorer Christopher Columbus discovered America.

Evidence file

Did a Scot reach America before Christopher Columbus? Here is some evidence to support this theory:

(1) The chapel at Roslin, where the Sinclair earls are buried, has rich carvings of various plants, including New World species like maize and American cactus.

(2) Rock-carvings at Westford, Massachusetts, USA, show a 14th-century long-ship and a medieval knight apparently bearing the armorial shield (see above) of the clan Gunn. Sir James Gunn is said to have been with Sinclair on his trip, and to have died in America. Archaeologists date the rock carvings to 600 years old.

(3) Micmac Indians have legends about 'men from over the sea'.

(4) Niccolo Zeno's own maps and story of the journey.

What do you think about all this evidence?

... in Scotland

Left: The Chapel at Roslin was the burial place of the Sinclair earls.

Below: A North Sea oil platform.

In 1468 the Scots king, James III, married the king of Denmark's daughter. As a wedding dowry from Denmark, James III received the Orkney and Shetland Islands.

The Viking language of the Northern Isles, called **Norn**, lived on until the 18th century. But after 1468 the main outside influence on the Northern Isles was Scottish not Norwegian – in the shape of settlers, administrators and churchmen, laws, language and culture. Norwegian law was abolished in Shetland in 1611.

Visitors to today's Northern Isles will see and hear plenty of evidence that these 'newest' parts of Scotland have kept strong Scandinavian links. Perhaps that's not surprising when you remember that they were Norse communities for over 700 years – longer than they have been Scottish.

Today North Sea oil is a resource shared mainly between Norway and Scotland. The deep-water drilling and service industries that extract the oil remind us of the shared maritime traditions of the Scots and the Norwegians.

ANSWERS

Page 3: **Take the test** – No. Some 19th-century artists in Sweden portrayed Vikings in this way, but in fact horns on helmets would have been dangerous to the Viking fighting next to you!

Page 3: **Take the test** – No. Vikings, as this book will show you, were known as more than pirates or raiders – they were also farmers, settlers and craftsmen.

Page 5: **Activity** – In order of importance: fresh water to avoid thirst; warm clothes to keep warm in an open boat; bread to eat; barrels for storage; swords for attacking on arrival in Scotland; animals for fresh milk and meat; axe and flints for cutting wood and making fires; fruit for vitamins; jewellery for looking good. These are only suggestions.

Page 5: **Activity** – What might a Viking do with a mobile phone or a computer, for example? Would such items be of any use in his or her world?

Page 7: **Mystery objects** – Object **A** on the left is a boatstem or stempost (AD 900-1000), one end of possibly a Viking boat. It was found buried in peat at Laig, Isle of Eigg. Made out of oak wood, the edge is stepped to allow for the fitting of the side timbers. Because Viking boats have a shallow draught (the level to which the boat sinks in the water), they could land on the shore and were well suited to sailing along coasts. Object **B** on the right, from Westness, Rousay, is called a 'chafing piece'. Made from deer antler (AD 800-1000), it was used for guiding fishing line over the side of the ship to stop the line rubbing (chafing) the wood when hauling in the catch.

Page 9: **Mystery object** – This is part of a stone cross-slab which would have been carved at the time the Vikings were in Shetland. The slab shows a horseman with a hooded clergyman on one side, and a book satchel on the other. The animals on the stone are a lion and possibly a boar.

Page 9: **Compass game**
Norway – E1 – D1 – D2 – C2 – Orkney
Orkney – C2 – B2 – B3 – Isle of Man
Isle of Man – B3 – B4 – C4 – C5 – Normandy

Page 11: **Mystery object** – This is the hilt (handle) of a gilt brass sword, decorated with animal and geometric patterns. It is very ornate and would have been used to show off the owner's wealth and power, because it is too delicate to have been used in an actual battle.

Page 13: **Mystery man** – This is one of twelve 'warders' known to have been amongst a hoard of 93 chesspieces found at Uig Bay on Lewis. The walrus ivory pieces were made in Iceland or Norway in the second half of the 12th century. The group is known as 'The Lewis chessmen'. The picture shows the warder wearing a helmet and a thick padded coat, holding a sword. He is biting the shield in the manner of a Norse 'berserker' (see also page 18).

Page 13: **Looking good** – Look out for the head of a wolf at the base of the brooch; it's looking downwards.

Page 15: **Mystery objects** – The first object (top) is a comb made from bone or antler, decorated with lines and pattern. These may seem like everyday items to us, but they were important enough to be buried with their owners. The other object is a heckle, used to prepare flax fibres for making cloth. The long spikes were designed to strip flax fibres and make them ready for spinning.

Page 17: **What's in a name?** –
Odin's day is Wednesday; Thor's day is Thursday; Frigga's day is Friday

Page 18: **Mystery object** – This charm is made from a bear's tooth and has the first six letters of the runic alphabet on it.

Page 19: **Code-breaker** – The runes spell the word 'Viking'

Page 26: **Mystery animal** – The creature may be a dragon; no one is certain. They probably didn't expect to meet a real dragon on their way to the Holy Land; it is a religious symbol of paganism being killed by the sword of Christianity.

Page 29: **Activity** – If you 'pay through the nose' for something, then you pay too much for it. The expression comes from the 'nose-tax' imposed by the Vikings in Dublin – the people who didn't pay the Viking taxes had their noses slit and were told to pay a fine!

Page 31: **Activity** – Today Ireland is the Republic of Ireland in the South, and Northern Ireland is part of the United Kingdom. All the islands off the coast of Scotland are part of the United Kingdom. The Holy Roman Empire is today split into a number of different countries: Germany, Austria, Switzerland, Liechtenstein, Luxemburg, the Czech Republic, Slovenia, Belgium, Netherlands and parts of Poland, France and Italy. Normandy now belongs to France.

Page 35: **Fast fact** – The death of Alexander III and the Maid of Norway was disastrous for Scotland because until there was a new King or Queen on the throne of Scotland, King Edward I of England was set to invade Scotland. Thus began the Scottish Wars of Independence.

WEBSITES TO VISIT

National Museums Scotland
www.nms.ac.uk

BBC
www.bbc.co.uk

British Museum
www.britishmuseum.co.uk

Jorvik Viking Centre, York
www.jorvik-viking-centre.co.uk

Visit Shetland
www.visitshetland.com

Historic Scotland
www.historic-scotland.gov.uk

National Museum of Ireland
www.museum.ie

Viking Ship Museum, Denmark
www.vikingeskibsmuseet.dk

Below: A 'Junior Jarl' aboard his galley in Lerwick during the 'Up Helly Aa' new year fire festival in Shetland.
(Scottish Life Archive: © Trustees of the National Museums of Scotland)

PLACES OF INTEREST

EDINBURGH: National Museum of Scotland – fine displays of settlements, burials, hoards and metalwork, including many items recovered from the Westness cemetery, Jarlshof, Broch of Birsay and Balnakeil. Some of the Lewis chessmen are in the medieval section.

GLASGOW: Hunterian Museum, University of Glasgow – displays include a Viking-age bronze balance found on Gigha.

IONA: Viking-age burial sites – a defensive earth-work around the abbey is still visible.

LARGS:
- 'Vikingar!' Museum and Visitor Centre: An informative and entertaining audio-visual presentation.
- Largs Viking Festival: usually takes place in the first two weeks of September. Events include re-enactment of the Battle of Largs, replica Viking villages, firework displays, long-ship burnings, *etc.*
- Pencil Monument: a round tower marks the site of the battle of Largs in 1263.

ORKNEY MAINLAND:
- St Magnus Cathedral, Kirkwall.
- Shrine of St Magnus, with Bishop's Palace where Haakon and the Maid of Norway probably spent their last days.
- The St Magnus Festival in June.
- Tankerness House Museum, Kirkwall: displays from Scar excavations, including the whalebone plaque.

BIRSAY (ORKNEY):
Extensive archaeological island site on the Brough of Birsay. Remains of later Bishop's and Earl's Palaces on the mainland opposite. Maes Howe burial mound with Viking runic graffiti. Ring of Brodgar (standing stones), six miles south, also has Viking graffiti.

ISLAND OF ROUSAY (ORKNEY): Westness Viking-age cemetery excavated in the 1970s and 1980s, with Norse settlement close by. Old cemetery mixed in with earlier Pictish graves. Here, in 1963, the fine Westness Brooch was found.

ISLAND OF WYRE (ORKNEY): Cubbie Roo's Castle, a Norse stronghold of the early 12th century which is the first known stone-built castle in Scotland. Named after the Norse merchant and farmer Kolbein Hruga for whom it was built.

ROSLIN: Rosslyn Collegiate Chapel, Roslin village, Midlothian. Some of the stone-carved decorations seem to include maize and American cactus, in a church built in 1446, almost 50 years before transatlantic voyage of Christopher Columbus. Sinclair earls of Orkney are buried in the crypt.

ROTHESAY: Rothesay Castle – a royal castle built *c.*1200 by King Alexander I to defend his country against the Norsemen. Fell to a Norse siege, *c.*1230.

SHETLAND:
- 'Up Helly Aa' Fire Festival, Lerwick, late January: celebration of local Norse traditions, with spectacular boat-burning ceremony.
- Extensive Viking archaeological site (Jarlshof).

WICK: Castle of Old Wick – a Norse stronghold of the 12th century, thought to have been built by Earl Rognvald.

Scotland's Vikings
Things to do

This picture was coloured in by:

Write your name here in runes (see next page for more details).

Code-breakers

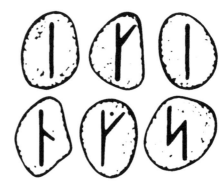

Use the Runic alphabet to make up some codes for your friends.

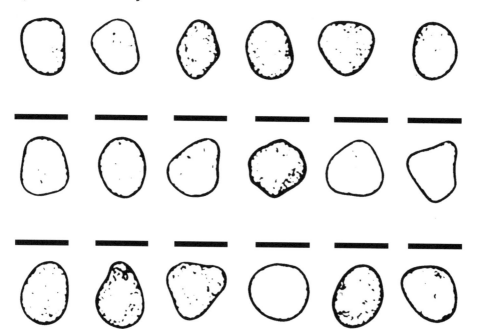

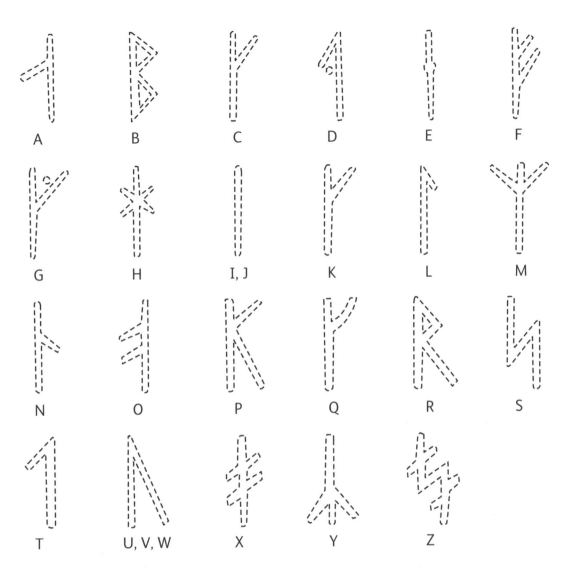

A   B   C   D   E   F

G   H   I, J   K   L   M

N   O   P   Q   R   S

T   U, V, W   X   Y   Z

Make your own rune stones

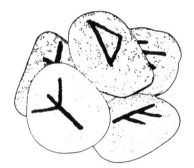

1. Trace the outline of the runes (above) and colour the letters in.

2. Find some small round smooth pebbles and paint each one with a different rune. Now make some words.

Long-ships

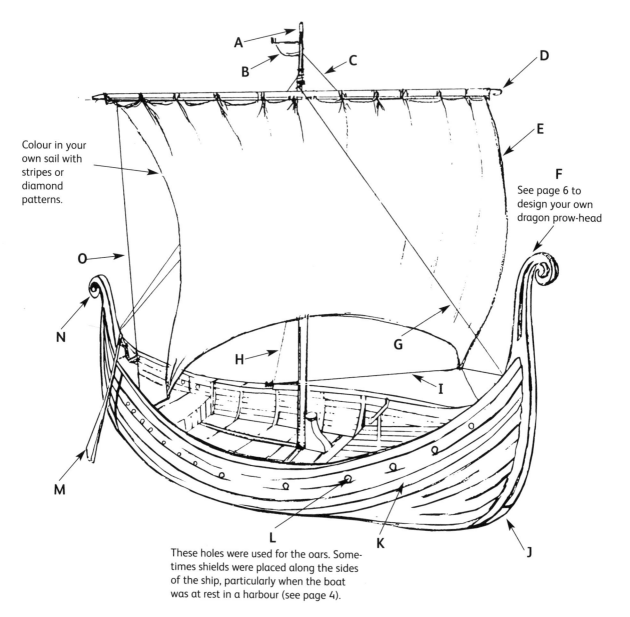

Colour in your own sail with stripes or diamond patterns.

F
See page 6 to design your own dragon prow-head

These holes were used for the oars. Sometimes shields were placed along the sides of the ship, particularly when the boat was at rest in a harbour (see page 4).

Can you learn all the names of the parts of a long-ship?

Colour in the picture.

A – mast	F – prow-head	L – oarport
B – weather vane	G – forestay	M – steerboard
C – halyard	H – backstay	N – sternpost
D – yard	I – sheet	O – shroud
E – sail	J – prow	
	K – strakes	

Word search

Parts of a Viking long-ship

Y	A	T	S	K	C	A	B	B	R	R	A
S	R	O	T	R	Y	A	R	D	E	R	A
M	R	S	E	L	A	S	M	R	P	K	W
U	E	T	E	E	T	S	M	A	R	R	A
D	F	O	R	E	S	T	A	Y	B	R	E
D	O	T	B	O	O	W	S	L	F	K	Y
P	U	T	O	S	P	O	T	A	S	O	S
T	B	O	A	R	M	R	R	H	I	Y	D
A	L	O	R	R	E	P	A	O	O	L	A
A	E	E	D	H	T	K	K	O	A	B	A
U	W	O	N	O	S	L	E	E	K	O	D
T	D	U	T	E	E	H	S	T	R	L	A

Move diagonally, as well as up and down, in any direction, to find the following words:

backstay	sail
forestay	sheet
halyard	shroud
keelson	steerboard
mast	stempost
oarport	strakes
prow	yard

Viking place names

R	Y	B	B	E	C	R	I	I	C	N	Y
N	A	Y	J	H	G	N	Y	B	R	I	L
Y	S	Y	U	U	H	O	C	P	E	A	E
A	N	H	S	M	R	N	Y	R	L	E	I
S	O	P	A	B	B	A	Y	E	E	L	E
D	L	A	R	I	S	A	I	G	R	O	A
L	O	C	K	E	R	B	I	E	W	N	A
A	C	R	H	T	N	L	K	C	I	W	C
N	S	T	S	O	S	R	Y	A	C	E	K
O	O	E	N	A	Y	Y	E	N	K	R	O
R	W	A	Y	B	A	D	O	A	Y	W	T
K	C	I	D	O	R	B	O	L	E	C	E

Arisaig	Lockerbie
Brodick	Orkney
Canonbie	Pabbay
Colonsay	Ronaldsay
Egilsay	Rothesay
Humbie	Westray
Jura	Wick
Lerwick	

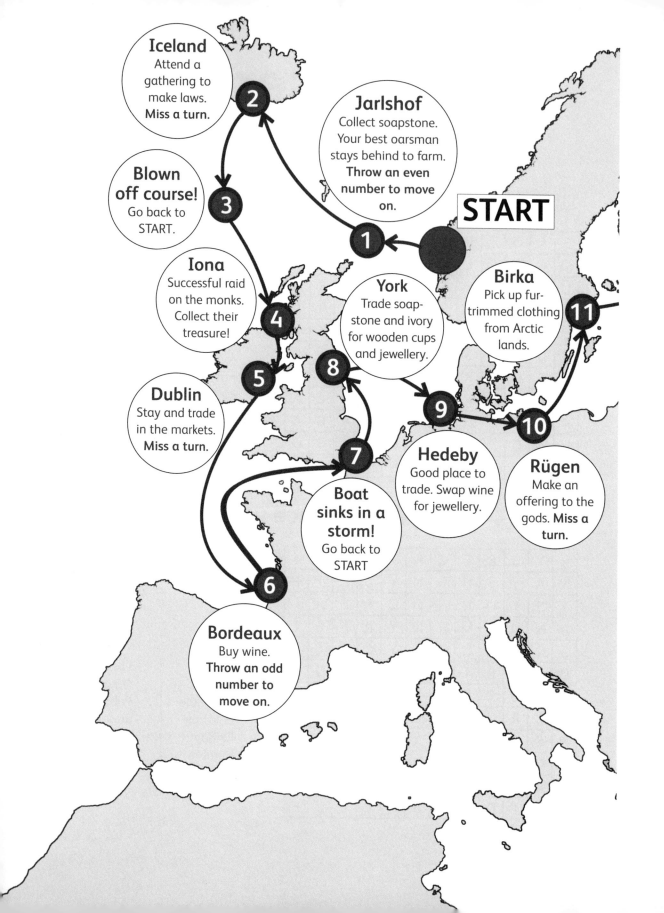

Viking journey

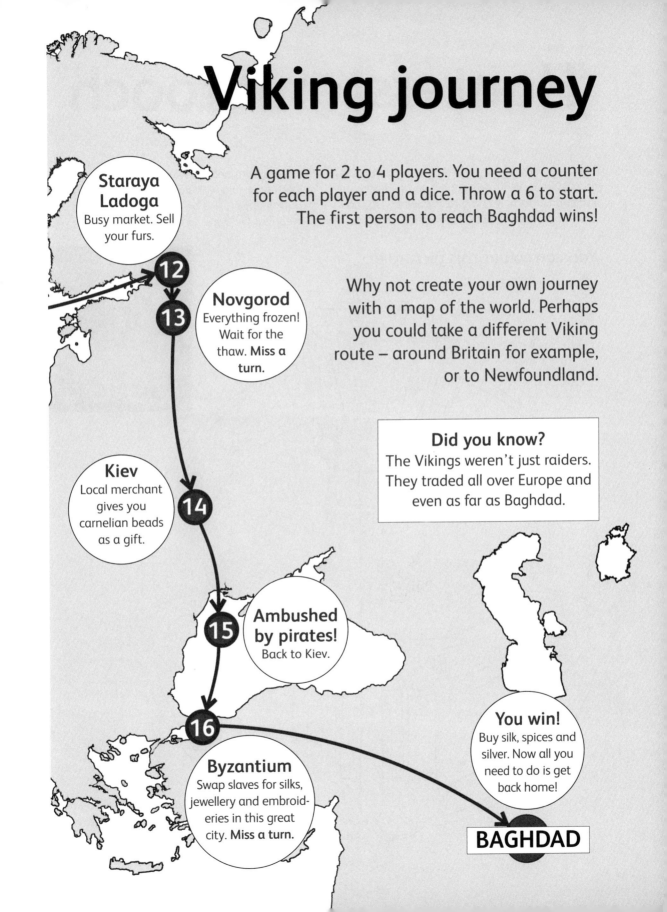

Staraya Ladoga
Busy market. Sell your furs.

12

13

Novgorod
Everything frozen! Wait for the thaw. **Miss a turn.**

Kiev
Local merchant gives you carnelian beads as a gift.

14

15

Ambushed by pirates!
Back to Kiev.

16

Byzantium
Swap slaves for silks, jewellery and embroideries in this great city. **Miss a turn.**

You win!
Buy silk, spices and silver. Now all you need to do is get back home!

BAGHDAD

A game for 2 to 4 players. You need a counter for each player and a dice. Throw a 6 to start. The first person to reach Baghdad wins!

Why not create your own journey with a map of the world. Perhaps you could take a different Viking route – around Britain for example, or to Newfoundland.

Did you know?
The Vikings weren't just raiders. They traded all over Europe and even as far as Baghdad.

Hunterston Brooch

This is the 8th-century Hunterston brooch, found in Ayrshire in 1830. Although it is an early Christian brooch, it had a Norse owner. On the back of the brooch are Viking runic inscriptions that date from between AD 900 and 1000. Made of silver and gold with amber settings, this is a beautiful object. It is on view in the National Museum of Scotland.

You can colour this picture in.

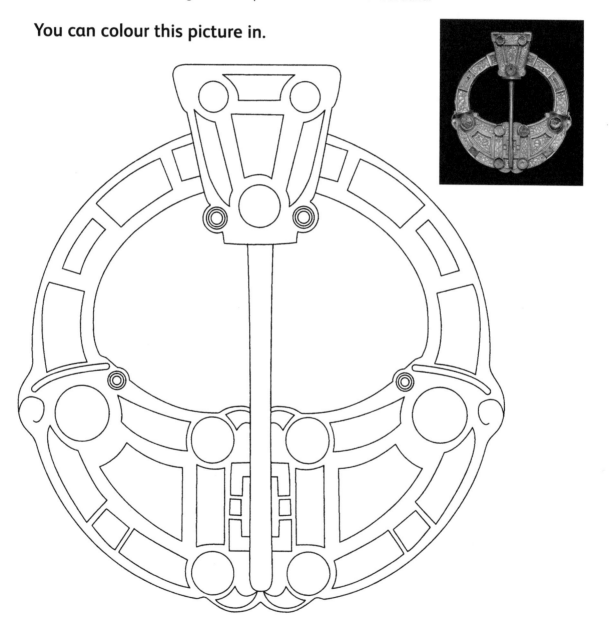